Note to Parents and Teachers

The READING ABOUT: STARTERS series introduces key science vocabulary to young children while encouraging them to discover and understand the world around them. The series works as a set of graded readers in three levels.

LEVEL 1: BEGINNING TO READ follows guidelines set out in the National Curriculum for Year 1 in schools. These books can be read alone or as part of guided or group reading. Each book has three sections:

• Information pages that introduce new words. These key words appear in bold throughout the book for easy recognition.
• A lively story that recalls this vocabulary and encourages children to use these words when they talk and write.
• A quiz and word search ask children to look back and recall what they have read.

PAWS, TAILS and WHISKERS looks at ANIMAL BODIES. Below are some activities related to the questions on the information spreads that parents, carers and teachers can use to discuss and develop further ideas and concepts:

p. 5 *A bird flies. How do the other animals move?* Encourage children to use specific words, e.g. slither, flap, wriggle, and to identify which parts help the animal to move.

p. 7 *Can your feet grab as well as your hands?* Ask children to compare their bodies with monkeys and other animals with feet or tails that grip, e.g. raccoon, bird.

p. 9 *Which parts of your body help you swim?* You could approach this by asking children to think about which parts don't help, e.g. ears!

p. 11 *Why do birds have feathers?* Extend discussion to include flight, keeping warm, keeping dry and perhaps even display (e.g. peacock). Compare with human skin/hair.

p. 13 *What would you look like without bones? A jellyfish?* Ask children to think about how bones give some animals their shape as well as thinking of animals without bones.

p. 15 *What animals would you like to stroke?* Ask children to imagine what it's like to feel different animals, e.g. snake (dry, smooth), snail (smooth, slimy) and hedgehog (prickly).

p. 17 *Why do big ears and big eyes help night animals?* Discuss how animals use their senses to find their way at night. You could include smell and touch too.

p. 19 *Shut your eyes. Can you tell food from its smell?* Try a blindfold taste test!

p. 21 *Feel your teeth. Why are some sharp and pointed?* Ask children to think about different foods they eat and how different teeth are good for chewing or biting.

ADVISORY TEAM

Educational Consultant
Andrea Bright – Science Co-ordinator, Trafalgar Junior School, Twickenham

Literacy Consultant
Jackie Holderness – former Senior Lecturer in Primary Education, Westminster Institute, Oxford Brookes University

Series Consultants
Anne Fussell – Early Years Teacher and University Tutor, Westminster College, Oxford Brookes University

David Fussell – C.Chem., FRSC

CONTENTS

© Aladdin Books Ltd 2004

Designed and produced by
Aladdin Books Ltd
2/3 Fitzroy Mews
London W1T 6DF

First published in
Great Britain in 2004 by
Franklin Watts
96 Leonard Street
London EC2A 4XD

A catalogue record for this
book is available from the
British Library.

ISBN 0 7496 5591 7

Printed in UAE

All rights reserved

Editor: Sally Hewitt

Design: Flick, Book Design
and Graphics

Picture research:
Brian Hunter Smart

Thanks to:
• The pupils of Trafalgar Infants
School, Twickenham for
appearing as models in this book.
• Lynne Thompson for helping
to organise the photoshoots.
• The pupils and teachers of
Trafalgar Junior School,
Twickenham and St. Nicholas
C.E. Infant School, Wallingford,
for testing the sample books.

Photocredits:
*l-left, r-right, b-bottom, t-top,
c-centre, m-middle*
Front cover tl & tr, 12b, 19t, 23tr
— Corel. Front cover tm & b, 3,
4, 13b, 14, 15tr, 17t, 19mr, 24 -28
all, 32tl, 32mlb — Comstock. 2tl,
6 both, 7l, 8t, 11t, 15m, 16t, 18br,
20t, 21t, 31tr, 31ml, 31mr, 32tr,
32mlt, 32mrb — Digital Stock.
2ml, 5bl, 5mr, 5br, 10t, 21ml, 22
both, 32mlc, 32mrc, 32bl, 32br —
John Foxx Images. 2bl, 17br, 23b,
29 both, 30 both, 31bl — Otto
Rogge Photography. 5t, 16br —
Flick Smith. 7r, 12tr — Jim Pipe.
8br, 9br, 11br, 13tr, 20mr —
Stockbyte. 9t, 32mrt — Dr James
P. McVey/NOAA. 10br — Corbis.
18t — PBD.

ANIMAL BODIES

Paws, Tails and Whiskers

by Jim Pipe

Aladdin/Watts
London • Sydney

You have a **body**.

Every animal has a **body** too.

Some animals are like you. You have two eyes and two ears. A dog does too!

Are these animals like you?
A worm has no legs.
A fish has no legs.
A bird has wings.
A snail has a shell.

Worm

Fish

Bird

Snail

• A bird flies. How do the other animals move?

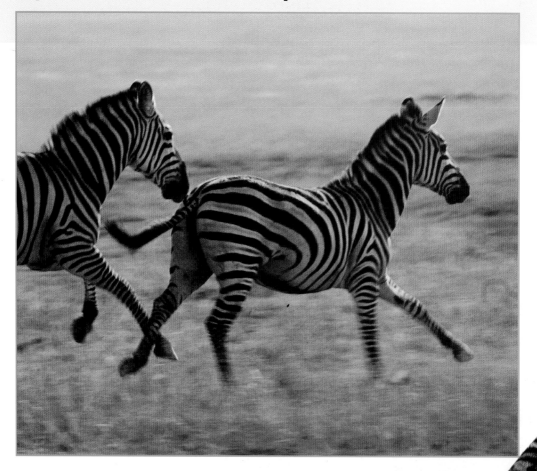

You have two legs and two feet. A zebra has four legs. Its feet are **hooves**.

A tiger has four legs. Its feet are **paws**.

6

A monkey's **paws** are like hands.
Its **tail** grabs like a hand too.

A monkey swings from
tree to tree. Can you?

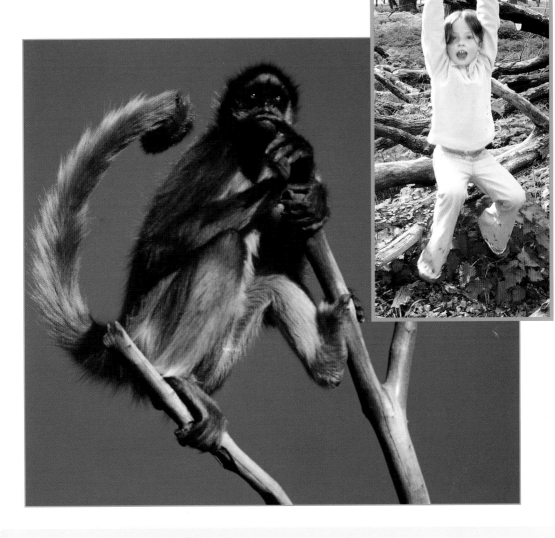

• Can your feet grab as well as your hands?

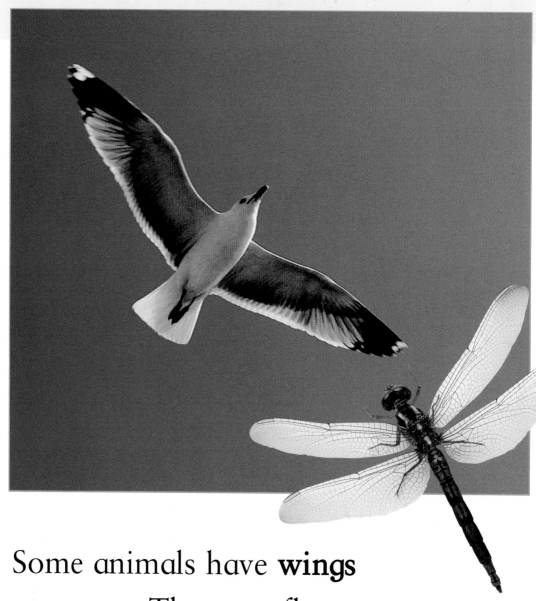

Some animals have **wings**
not arms. They can fly.

A bird has two **wings**.
A dragonfly has four **wings**.

8

Sea animals have tails not legs.
Their tails push them along.

A seal steers
with its **flippers**.

A fish steers
with its **fins**.

• Which parts of your body help you swim?

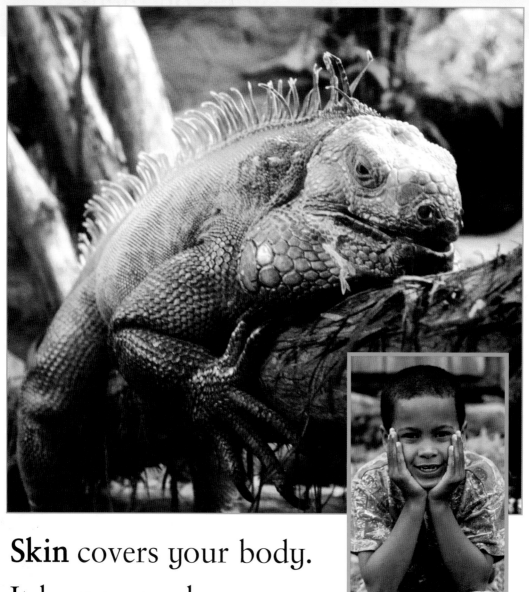

Skin covers your body.
It keeps you dry.

Your **skin** feels soft. A lizard's **skin** feels rough. It is made of **scales**.

10

Fish have smooth **scales** on their skin. Birds have **feathers**.

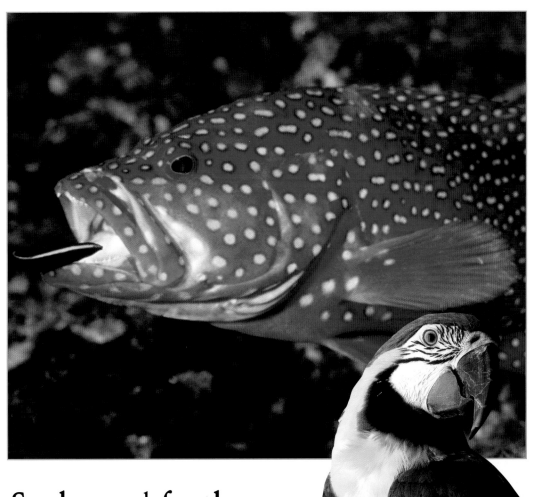

Scales and **feathers** can be bright colours.

• *Why do birds have feathers?*

Bones protect your insides.
They give you your shape.
Can you feel them?

Many animals have
bones too. Bird **bones**
are light for flying.

12

A crab has no **bones**.
A hard **shell** protects it.

A tortoise has
bones and a **shell**
on its back.

• What would you look like without bones? A jellyfish?

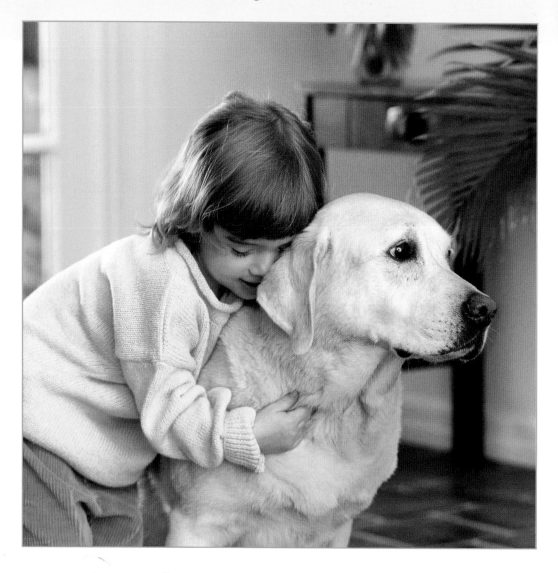

You have **hair** on your head.
A dog has **hairy fur** all over its body.

Fur keeps an animal warm in winter.

14

A cat has long **hairs** on its face. These are **whiskers**.

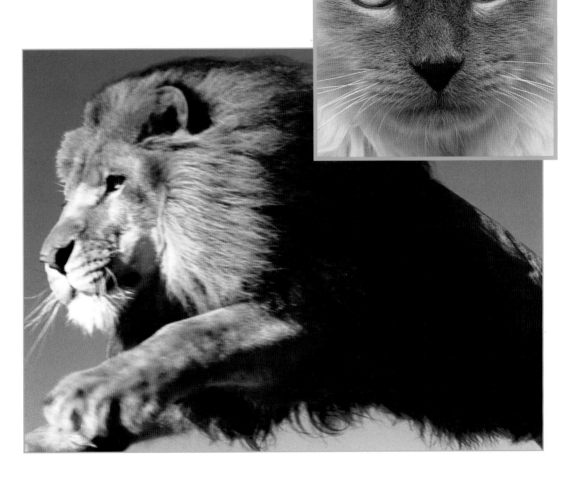

This lion has long **hairs** on his head. This is his **mane**.

• *What animals would you like to stroke?*

Like you, animals see with their **eyes**.
A whale's **eye** is as big as a football.

A snail has **eyes** at the end
of its **tentacles**.

Like you, animals hear with their **ears**.
A rabbit's long **ears** hear quiet sounds.

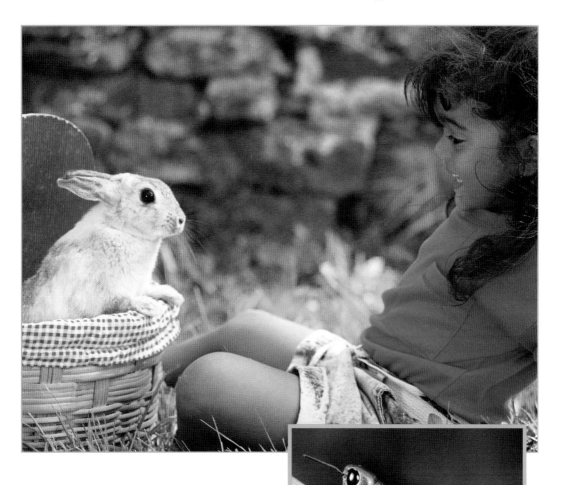

A grasshopper has
ears in its knees!

• Why do big ears and big eyes help night animals?

Animals smell with their **nose**.
A pig sniffs for food on the ground.

An elephant's **trunk**
is a long **nose**.
It grabs like
a hand!

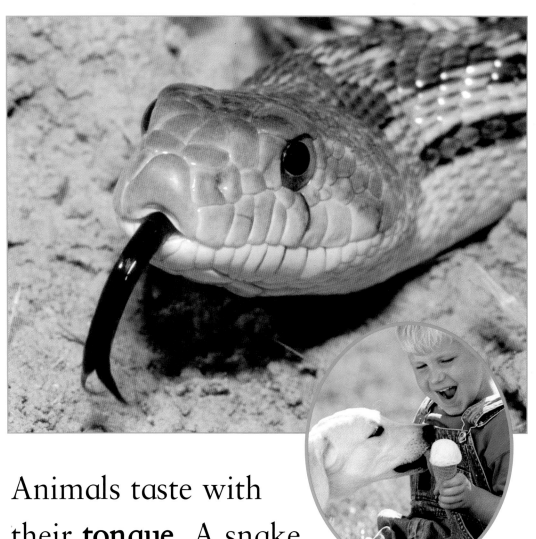

Animals taste with their **tongue**. A snake smells with it too!

Animals lick food with their **tongue**. A dog has a long **tongue**.

• Shut your eyes. Can you tell food from its smell?

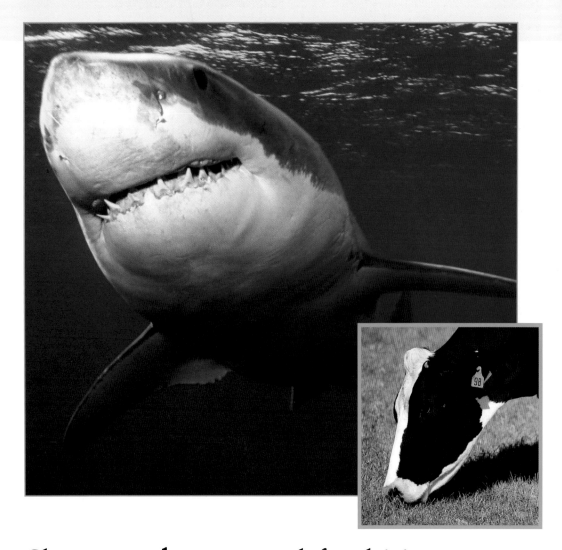

Sharp **teeth** are good for biting.
A shark has lots of sharp **teeth**. Crunch!

Bumpy **teeth** are good for chewing.
A cow chews grass all day. Munch!

A hippopotamus has two long **teeth**. These are its **tusks**.

Birds do not have **teeth**. They grab food with their **beak**.

• Feel your teeth. Why are some sharp and pointed?

Many animals have parts you don't.

Do you have **claws**?
A crab has **claws**.
Watch out, they pinch!

Do you have a **horn**? A rhino has **horns** on its head.

Watch out, it butts!

Do you have prickly **spines**?
A porcupine has **spines**. Watch out,
they are sharp!

A wasp has a **sting**
in its tail. Don't
make it angry!

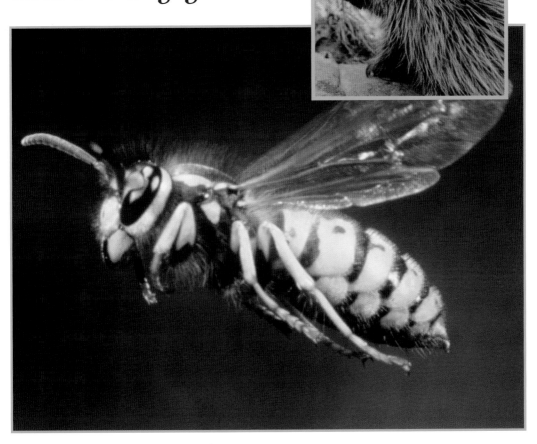

• What other animals have parts you don't?

Now read the story of **My New Pet.** Look out for words about **animals**.

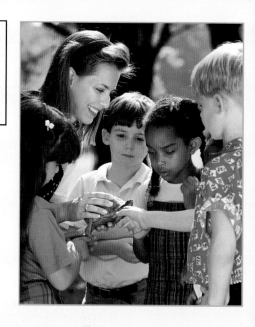

Today we can bring
a pet to school.
I have no pet.
I want one too!

Asha has a cat called Charlie.
I'd like a cat too.
Charlie has soft **fur** and long **whiskers**.
Ouch! His **paws** have sharp **claws**.

Dave brings Goldie, his dog.
I'd like a dog too.
Goldie sniffs with his **nose**.
Dave gives him a biscuit.

Goldie wags his **tail**.
He sticks out his big **tongue.**
We all laugh.

Ming has a tortoise. His name is Speedy. He moves VERY slowly.

Speedy has a tough **skin** and a smooth **shell**.

We all look for Speedy's **ears**. Wow! A tortoise does not have any!

Ben shows us his goldfish, Moby. I like Moby's shiny gold **scales**.

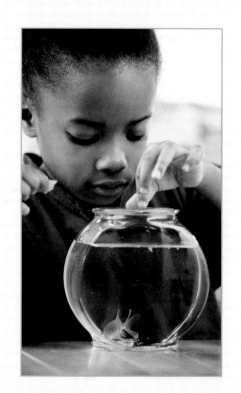

Moby flaps his **fins** up and down.

Moby has no **teeth**. He just swallows his food.

Charlie's **eyes** follow Moby. He would like to eat him!

Ally has a bird
called Barney.
He has white **feathers**.
"Look at his big **beak!**"
I say to Ally.

Ruth shows a picture of her pony, Rusty.
Rusty has a red **mane**.

I would like to ride Rusty.
His **hooves** go "clip-clop" on the road.

Tariq has a pet spider.
It is very **hairy**.
We count its legs.
A spider has eight legs!
It has eight **eyes** too.

I feel sad. I'd like a pet too.
My teacher says, "Come and look!"

It's a **hairy** caterpillar!
"We can watch it
grow," says my teacher.

One day, my caterpillar
will grow into a butterfly
with **wings**. Now it eats
and eats. Just like me!

Draw a picture of
your favourite animal.
Write labels to show
parts of its **body**.

Can you also draw
where it lives and
what it eats?

Tail

Ears

Paws

QUIZ

Which animal has **hooves?**

Answer on page 6

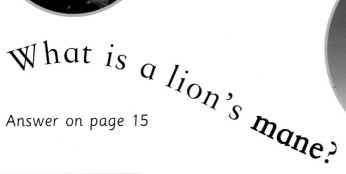

What covers a fish's **skin?**

Answer on page 11

What is a lion's **mane?**

Answer on page 15

Where are a grasshopper's **ears?**

Answer on page 17

Did you know the answers? Give yourself a

Do you remember these **animal** words?
Well done! Can you remember any more?

 body
page 4

paws
page 6

 wings
page 8

flippers
page 9

 scales
page 10

shell
page 13

 fur
page 14

trunk
page 18

 beak
page 21

horn
page 22